ROBERT JACOBE

# The Sellable House

*Tip for Selling Your House for the Most Money in Any Market*

First edition

This book was professionally typeset on Reedsy.
Find out more at reedsy.com

# Contents

# 1

# Introduction

Deciding to sell your house is a big decision. And while there's much to think about to make this happen, it doesn't have to be a complicated and overwhelming process, and in fact, can be really fun! The goal of every homeowner is to sell their house as quickly as possible for the most money. This happens when your house stands out from the competition and is priced correctly for the market. In our real estate company we call this creating **The Sellable House**, and we work with our clients to make this happen. Our goal? To help realize the full potential of the home and to make it stand out to potential buyers, so that you, the seller, receive the most money in the shortest amount of time. Now, you might be thinking "how do I make that happen"?

We have established a checklist of tips and strategies to help homeowners make their home marketable and extremely attractive to buyers. These tips and strategies will apply in any real estate market, regardless of where you live. While selling your home in a sellers market might not require implementation of all the tips, doing some of them can still make a difference to bring in a higher price in a shorter amount of time. When selling in a buyer's market, these strategies are crucial. These tips and strategies work together to put your best foot forward within your market, so that buyers can see your home's potential and how their life might fit within it. Let's talk about how to get your house sold!

The tips and strategies we will be discussing here are:

- Understanding your real estate market
- Real estate terms
- Finding potential issues and making repairs and/or upgrades
- Addressing curb appeal
- Decluttering & depersonalizing
- Cleaning
- Staging
- Removing valuables or potentially dangerous items
- Understanding home values

# 2

# Understanding Your Real Estate Market

### Tip #1:
### Understand Your Local Market

How much do you know about your local housing market? Is it a seller's market? A buyer's market? On average, how long does it take to sell a house in your local market? Do you know how to look for comparable properties to help you have an understanding of your home's market value? It's important that you understand which kind of market you're in so that you have a realistic view of the selling process.

Generally speaking, the **real estate market** is all of the houses for sale at any given time in a specific area. Different areas in cities may have differing markets. Some areas may be very desirable and sales happen quickly, while other areas may take longer to find the right buyer. Taking this a step further, in a **seller's market**, demand for housing exceeds the available supply. This is a benefit to sellers, as buyers don't have as many options to choose from, and generally are less picky about features and conditions. This market may also produce multiple offers to buy your house, making the process more challenging but also more fun. Conversely, in a ***buyer's market***, supply exceeds demand, switching the advantage to buyers, allowing them the option to be more choosy about features and conditions. A buyer's market will demand that you put your best foot forward and make your home sellable or risk not selling or having to sell at a lower price.

While it's important to understand the kind of market you're working with, these tips and strategies will work in any market to help make your house stand out from the rest. In a seller's market, it may not be necessary to do as much to make your house marketable and attractive to buyers, because fewer available houses drive up demand. In this type of market buyers are more willing to overlook things in the hopes of getting an accepted offer. In a buyer's market, though, you will need to step it up to make your house stand out from the crowd of other houses that are available. Buyers have a lot more to choose between, and homes that are in excellent condition with modern updates will attract buyers over homes that come with many needed improvement projects. Homes that are in need of repairs will also generally receive offers with more contingencies that must be satisfied prior to closing. Understanding the housing market in your area will provide you with a realistic view of what buyers will be expecting, the average length of time it might take to sell your house, and your home's value as compared to others in your area.

There are many resources available online that can help you with this process. To find information about current home prices in your area, check websites such as Zillow.com, Trulia.com, Redfin.com or any local real estate broker website. Also, many of the local multiple listing real estate services are accessible to the general public and will have much data on local real estate sales. The websites also have pictures of current homes for sale, which you can use to compare to the condition of your house, as well as any upgrades you might need to consider to stand out from your competition.

**Key Takeaway:**
**Understand how the market you are in will affect home sales.**

# 3

# Real Estate Terminology

### Tip #2:
### Know Your Real Estate Terms

H aving a basic knowledge of real estate terminology is really beneficial when going through the process of selling your house. You will be working with a variety of different people and businesses throughout the steps of a home sale; including, agents/brokers, lenders, inspectors, appraisers, and escrow agents, to name a few. Understanding each of their roles, as well as their 'lingo', can eliminate confusion and misunderstandings. The following are some basic real estate terms to help you better understand the process as you go through it. This is not a complete list of real estate terms, but we've included those that pertain to this topic.

**Appraisal:** A professional analysis used to determine the value of a property; performed by a licensed appraiser. This is usually paid for by the buyer as part of their lender's requirement.

**Closing:** The completion of a financial transaction.

**Contingency:** A clause in a real estate sales agreement that must be satisfied before closing can occur.

**Comparable Property**: Also referred as a comp, current homes for sale that are most similar to yours.

**Days on Market:** Also referred to as DOM, the number of days a house has been for sale, or the total number of days from listing through closing of a property.

**FSBO**: For Sale by Owner; someone who sells their house without the help of a real estate professional.

**Home Inspection:** A limited, visual examination of the condition of a property, performed by a licensed home inspector. This is usually paid for by the buyer, and is to the buyer's benefit.

**Market Value:** The current value of your home based on what a ready and willing purchaser would pay.

**Principal Real Estate Broker:** A real estate broker who has additional education and experience and supervises other brokers/agents.

**Real Estate:** Real property, including land and any permanent buildings on it, whether natural or man made.

**Real Estate Agent/Real Estate Broker**: a state licensed professional who represents buyers or sellers of real estate.

**Realtor:** Someone who belongs to the National Association of Realtors; brokers and agents are not required to be a member to be licensed and practice real estate.

**Staging:** Preparing a home for sale, and can involve redecorating, rearranging furniture, and cleaning to present the home in the best possible way.

**Key Takeaway:**
**Learn the lingo. Understand what the people involved with the sale**
**of your house are talking about.**

# 4

# Making Repairs and/or Upgrades

**Tip #3:**
**Take an honest look at your house and determine if there are repairs and/or upgrades that should be made before putting it up for sale.**

Repairs and/or upgrades are something that we talk a lot about with our clients. Houses go through a lot of wear and tear as they age, from the weather, and as people live in them, and oftentimes it is absolutely to your benefit to fix things before trying to sell. Repairs and upgrades can often have a significant return on their investment, making your house a more attractive option for buyers. Making repairs prior to listing your house might also lead to fewer contingencies from a buyer when making an offer, since you've already taken care of those things they might want repaired before closing. This can lead to a shorter length of time to closing a sale.

When considering *repairs*, think in terms of "broken" or "worn out". And this includes big things and small ones. Is the roof damaged or at the end of its expected life? How about the furnace and hot water heater? Do all the appliances work correctly? What about that toilet that runs all the time? Consider having a home inspection done by a professional home inspector to help identify potential issues. This report will show you some of the key repairs needed in your home, or repairs that could come up at a later date. This will give you a chance to fix known problems, and remove any potential future issues before they happen, or at least have the knowledge of their existence.

*In need of repair*

*Ready for sale*

Some things to look at when considering repairs:

- Does everything that comes with the house work correctly? Lighting (including working light bulbs), appliances, plumbing, electrical, furnace, A/C and water heater?
- Are there fireplaces and do they work correctly? Are they clean and maintained?
- Are there, or have there been any leaks? If so, were they professionally fixed and do you have documentation?
- Have any windows lost their seal? Do windows and doors close and lock properly?

When thinking about *upgrades*, focus on out-of-date, older aspects of your home. Are your counter tops still 1970's formica?

Does the bathroom still have a 1980's wallpaper border? Do you have old vinyl or tile flooring or shabby carpet that has definitely seen better days? How about the condition and color of the paint? Making upgrades to these types of items means that your buyer won't have to. And that makes your house a much more desirable option for them.

Most buyers want a house to be move-in ready; they don't usually have the time or additional funds to take on a number of fix-it projects. So step back and try to take a long, honest look at the condition of your home and what could or should be repaired or upgraded, within a budget that works for you. Focus on the areas of the home that matter the most to potential buyers: kitchen, primary suite, and family gathering rooms. Some types of repairs or remodeling require plans and permits, so consider hiring a professional to help with these. Also consider upgrades that focus on energy efficiency and smart home features, both which add value to a home from a buyer's perspective. An upgraded house in good condition will almost always sell faster and bring in a higher price than one that needs some work.

*Outdated furnishings and decor.*

*Simple and updated for potential buyers*

The following are some interesting statistics on how repairing and upgrading homes can affect their resale value. The cost of projects like these may not be feasible, but you can understand how something as simple as repainting your front door or upgrading some appliances can increase the desirability of your home. Note that buyers have a certain expectation for the condition and features of a house. For example, vinyl, double paned windows are an expectation today versus being considered an upgrade. Things of this nature that a home may lack will most likely result in a decreased market value and a lower sale price. According to Remodeling Magazine, here are some home renovation projects and how much you could expect to recoup.

| Project | Cost Recouped |
|---|---|
| Stone veneer | 102.7 % |
| Entry door replacement (steel) | 100.9% |
| Fiber cement siding replacement | 88.5% |
| Minor kitchen remodel | 85.7% |
| Vinyl window replacement | 68.5% |
| Mid-range bathroom remodel | 66.7% |
| Roof replacement | 61.1% |
| Composite deck addition | 39.8% |
| Major upscale kitchen remodel | 31.7% |
| Mid-range bathroom addition | 30.2% |
| Energy Efficient homes | Increase in value of 2-8% |
| Smart home features | Increase in value of 3-5% |

**Key Takeaway:**
**Consider making appropriate repairs and/or upgrades to make your house stand out from the crowd.**

# 5

# Curb Appeal

### Tip #4:
### Maximize Your Curb Appeal

As we've all heard, first impressions matter. And that goes for your house too! According to Investopedia.com, curb appeal is defined as "the general attractiveness of a house or other piece of property from the sidewalk to a prospective buyer." Buyers only get one chance to see your home for the first time, and you want them to be impressed. Maximizing your curb appeal makes buyers want to see more of your house, so don't skip this part. Stand in front of your house and take a good, unbiased look. And then consider the following:

- Is the siding, stone, or brick in good condition?
- Is the paint faded, peeling or cracked?
- Is the area leading up to your front door clean and unclut-

17

tered? Are there cobwebs in the corners?

· Are windows clean and in good condition, with no broken seals or cracks?

· Is the landscaping trimmed and weeded, with healthy plants, and a tidy spread of bark dust or mulch?

Take stock of these items and consider how, within your budget, you can maximize these things. It can be as simple as mowing the lawn, weeding the beds, sweeping the entry and perhaps pressure washing the house and hardscape surfaces such as concrete walks. Or a more ambitious plan might include a new exterior paint job in modern neutral colors, and completely replacing a cracked driveway. The key is to try and see your house from a stranger's point of view, and take steps to make it as universally appealing as possible. According to homelight.com, buyers will pay on average 7% more for a home with enhanced curb appeal.

Interestingly enough, the front door is a key focal point that can add or detract from your home's value. A recent study by zillow.com, "finds that homes with slate blue or black front doors appeal to more recent and prospective buyers and could sell for a higher price. Conversely, pale pink and cement gray front doors could negatively impact a home's value." Remember that your potential buyers only get one first impression, so make it a good one!

**Key Takeaway:**
**Make a great first impression!**

# 6

# Declutter and Depersonalize

### Tip #5:
### Declutter and Depersonalize Your House

Potential buyers need to be able to form an emotional connection to the house they choose to buy. They need to be able to see themselves living within the space. And what we find more often than not, when showing homes to prospective buyers, is that they can't do that if the home is "full of the current owner". When the home is full of personal items, or decorated in a very specific style, it's hard for a potential buyer to see past all of that to the house itself. We all tend to fill our homes with things we love: personal photographs, decor, knick-knacks and trinkets, collections... things that WE have an emotional connection with. When selling your home, you need to put those things away so that the buyer can imagine their own life in the house.

**Decluttering** means to remove unnecessary items. Look around your house, inside and out. How many things can you see that are unnecessary? Are there things that sit out because it's convenient or you've no place to put them? Too many books spilling out of the bookcase? Boxes of cereal on top of the fridge? Children's toys on the floor, or sports equipment laying around outside? These are all red flags that send a message to potential buyers that there's a lack of storage in the house. In reality, there may be plenty of storage available in the house, but these types of things make a buyer *feel* like things are crowded. Put unnecessary things away, and if you don't actually have enough space to do that, consider boxing them up in the garage or renting a storage unit until after the house is sold. Getting ready to put your house on the market is a great time to sort through and clean out things we no longer need. Your goal is to make your home appealing to a large number of people by presenting an orderly and functional place that feels calm and inviting. Think simple. Think less is more.

**Depersonalizing** means to remove the sense of a personal identity. You want your home to appeal to as many potential buyers as possible, and doing this involves removing your personal footprint from it. Family photographs, memorabilia, collectibles, items with your name on them, very specific decor (such as roosters everywhere, or a fussy victorian theme), and decor items that might not appeal to a large number of people (such as a deer head on the wall, or black wall paint) should all be removed. You should also consider removing religious items. "No matter how important faith is to you, you want your home to appeal to the widest array of buyers from all walks of life. Take down any religious art, statues, and relics, and replace them with something more neutral, like a plant or piece of art". One mistake sellers often make is thinking that removing personal items such as these takes away the character or personality of the house. In reality, these items reflect the character and personality of you, the owner. Leaving them in makes it much harder for buyers to make an emotional connection to the house and, as a result, they will often just move on. Remember that by decluttering and depersonalizing, you are not diminishing your likes or beliefs. You are just making your "for sale house" more attractive to a larger pool of people.

Depersonalizing doesn't mean removing all the decor. It's about making the decor more neutral so that a buyer can picture themselves in the space. When you take down the large family portrait, think about putting up a pretty botanical picture. Repaint color charged walls with a fresh coat of paint in a neutral color. Pack away your sports memorabilia collection. Think neutral. Think universally appealing.

*Too cluttered and disorganized*

*Uncluttered and organized.*

*Too much personalization and messy*

*Depersonalized and orderly*

**Key Takeaway:**
**Think simple. Think less is more.**
**Think neutral. Think universally appealing.**

# 7

# Clean Your House Inside and Out

### Tip #6:
### Clean, Clean, Clean

Tip number six is simple: a clean house is attractive and appealing, a dirty house is not. Clean your house, inside and out. Deep clean items that you don't do on a regular basis. A clean house exudes a feeling of care and affection for it, which a buyer instinctively picks up on. A dirty house is an instant put off, for a couple of reasons. First, it makes you feel that the house has been neglected, which can immediately make you wonder what else has been ignored. And second, it makes you feel like you don't want to connect to the house; it creates a barrier to really seeing it..

Also, take stock of how your house smells inside. We often can't smell any odors in our own homes because we're used to them. Bring in a trusted friend or relative and ask them what they smell when they walk in. Pets, mildew, and a myriad of other things can create odors in the home that we no longer notice.

It's important to find the cause of and neutralize these before buyers come through. When preparing for showings, it's always a plus to have your house smell nice. Candles, scented plug-ins or fresh flowers are a great option.

If time is a barrier to deep cleaning, consider hiring a cleaning company to do it. It is money well spent, and allows you to only have to focus on cleaning maintenance while the house is for sale.

**Area cleaning guidelines:**

Kitchen

- Dust/wash/polish cabinet doors and hardware
- Clean and disinfect sink, faucet and disposal
- Wash counter tops
- Clean inside and outside of all appliances
- Clean behind, under and on top of refrigerator
- Sweep and mop floors
- Wash windows
- Clean inside cabinetry where needed


Bathrooms

- Clean and disinfect toilets, tubs, showers, sinks and faucets
- Wash/polish cabinet doors
- Wash counter tops
- Sweep and mop floors
- Wash windows

- Wash bath mats and remove or replace dirty towels
- Clean inside of cabinetry where needed

## Bedrooms

- Make beds
- Sweep and mop, or vacuum flooring
- Dust and polish dressers, bookcases, woodwork, and decor
- Wash windows

## Family Gathering Rooms

- Dust and polish furniture, woodwork, decor, TVs
- Wash windows
- Straighten couch cushions, pillows, blankets
- Sweep and mop, or vacuum flooring

## Laundry Area

- Pull washer and dryer out and clean under and behind
- Sweep and mop
- Wipe down washer and dryer

## Miscellaneous

- Carpet: spot clean; vacuum; consider having it professionally cleaned

- Blinds: dust and/or wipe clean
- Curtains/drapes: wash or spot clean
- Walls: wash or dust as needed
- Woodwork and doors: wash or dust as needed
- Clean and sanitize light switches and door knobs

**Key Takeaway:**
**A clean house is A Sellable House.**

# 8

# Staging

**Tip #7:**
**Stage Your House to Give Buyers an**
**Emotional Connection**

According to the National Association of Realtors, staging "is about showcasing an engaging, move-in ready home that creates an emotional connection with the buyer." And in an article at Forbes.com, we find that when potential buyers come to view your home, they want to see themselves living there—to feel at home and not as if they're in someone else's house. Too many personal items around the house can be distracting, but completely bare rooms can also come off as cold and impersonal. Home staging can be the solution. Staging can increase a buyer's perceived value of a home, minimize negative aspects while maximizing positives, and also help buyers visualize what to do with extra or unusual spaces in the house.

You can stage your home yourself or hire a professional staging company to do it for you. The national average cost of home staging is just over $1,400.00, and it may be well worth your investment. According to a 2021 survey by the National Association of Realtors, "more than 80% of real estate agents representing buyers said staging made it easier for their buyers to see themselves in the home. And 23% of agents said that home staging led to increased offers between 1% and 5% compared to similar homes that weren't staged." That may not sound like much, but on a home priced at $500,000, an offer with an increase of 3% would be an additional $15,000. Additionally, according to HomeAdvisor, "homes that have been staged spend between 33% and 50% less time on the market." If you choose to do the staging yourself, think simple, light, bright, uncluttered, depersonalized, and on trend. Spend some time online looking at current decor trends, and implement some strategies to incorporate some of those ideas.

Staging should not be confused with decorating. Decorating is choosing furniture, paint colors and decor that appeal to you. Staging is giving the home a simplified, on-trend, temporary update that makes the home attractive to a large number of potential buyers. It can involve removing or rearranging furniture and decor you already have, or renting and bringing in completely new pieces. It could involve adding fresh, neutral paint colors, or even a partial or full remodel of an area in the house. It isn't necessary to stage the entire home; staging should focus on two or three of the key rooms buyers pay more attention to: kitchen, primary suite and family gathering spaces. Below are some photos of some nicely staged rooms.

**Key Takeaway:**
**Statistics show that staging helps**
**to sell your home faster and for more money.**

# 9

# Removing Valuables

**Tip #8:**
**Remove or Lock up Private, Valuable or**
**Potentially Dangerous Items.**

Before the house is available for showings, it's really important to remember to remove or lock up the following:

- Items of significant personal or monetary value
- Things that you want to keep private
- Anything that could pose a danger to people going through your home

These could include things such as:

- Jewelry
- Art

- Computers
- Photos
- Family heirlooms
- Financial, identity, or health information
- Weapons
- Tools
- Any number of other items that have a particular importance to you, or could pose a danger to someone.

We'd like to think, of course, that potential buyers are honest people with integrity. In reality, we know that there are people out there who are dishonest and will take advantage of an opportunity. So remove the opportunity. The length of time your house is for sale is a relatively short period in the whole scheme of things. It is much better to remove these types of items from your home than to leave them at risk. Better to be safe than sorry and protect those things that would be catastrophic to you if something happened to them or they went missing.

**Key Takeaway:**
**Don't allow buyers access to private, valuable or dangerous items.**

# 10

# Understand Pricing & Home Value

**Tip #9:**
**Price your house correctly from the beginning.**

The most important part of creating a sellable house is pricing it correctly for your market at the very beginning. The starting price influences how potential buyers view the house. Price it too high, and you'll lose out on very qualified buyers. Price it too low and you'll end up selling it for less than its value. Sellers obviously want the most money possible for their house, and some feel like there's nothing to lose with starting at a higher price. The price can always come down, right? In our experience, this can be an almost near fatal mistake. When a house is priced too high and sits on the market for an extended period of time, buyers begin to instinctively feel that there must be something wrong with it. And even future price reductions don't seem to change that dynamic. Therefore, it's really imperative that you have a realistic expectation for what your house is worth in your market, and price it accordingly.

There are multiple strategies for calculating the appropriate price range, including:

- Checking with an online automated valuation model (AVM)
- Hiring a real estate broker to perform a Comparative Market Analysis (CMA) or a Broker Price Opinion (BPO)
- Hiring an appraiser

An automated valuation model (AVM) is an online algorithm that uses available data to predict the value of your home. Zillow's Zestimate is one example. AVM's are a good starting point, but they are from perfect because the algorithm doesn't know all the specific details and condition of your home. Think of it as a ballpark number.

A Comparative Market Analysis, performed by a licensed broker or agent, is an in depth comparison of multiple homes that are as similar as possible to yours and that are located in your specific area. A CMA compiles data from homes that have recently sold as well as homes that are currently for sale, and can also consider how long the homes took to sell, or how long they have been for sale. This is a much more detailed report, that along with the local knowledge you'll gain by using a local broker, can offer much more detailed insight into an appropriate price. A Broker Price Opinion, or BPO, is a similar analysis and is also performed by a licensed broker. This is the most common form of determining home value prior to putting it up for sale.

Lastly, hiring a professional appraiser to perform a home appraisal will likely get you the most accurate value for your home. An appraiser will value your home through several different methods, as well as perform an in-person walk through of the home. This allows an appraiser to increase or decrease value based on the actual and unique condition of the home.


**Key Takeaway:**
**Price your home correctly from the start.**

# 11

# Conclusion

T hank you for reading this book, The Sellable House, about selling your house for the most money in the shortest amount of time in any market. We believe in these tips and strategies and have found them to be successful for our clients. We hope they provide some insight into the process and give you ideas for how to best present and market your home for sale. Good luck, and we wish you a fun and lucrative sale!

If you enjoyed this book and found the information interesting and valuable, we would appreciate a favorable review!

# 12

# Resources

Slate blue, black front doors can sell homes for as much as *$6,449 more - Jun 23, 2022*. (2022, June 23). Zillow MediaRoom. https://zillow.mediaroom.com/2022-06-23-SLATE-blue,-black-front-doors-can-sell-homes-for-as-much-as-6,449-more

Chen, J. (2021, June 10). *Curb appeal*. Investopedia. https://investopedia.com/terms/c/curb-appeal.asp

Bond, C. (2022, November 2). Is home staging worth it? *Forbes Advisor*. https://forbes.com/advisor/mortgages/is-home-staging-worth-it/

*Why staging matters, even in a seller's market*. (2021, September 17). www.nar.realtor. https://nar.realtor/blogs/styled-staged-sold/why-staging-matters-even-in-a-sellers-market

Sun-Tan, C., & Sun-Tan, C. (2023, August 24). How to depersonalize your house for sale without losing its charm. *HomeLight Blog*. https://homelight.com/blog/depersonalize-the-house/

Dellinger, A. (2022, August 23). *How to price your home for a perfect sale*. Bankrate. https://bankrate.com/real-estate/how-to-price-your-house-for-sale/#price

Beck, R. H. (2023, June 14). *Real estate terms and definitions.* Bankrate. https://bankrate.com/real-estate/real-estate-term s-and-definitions/

*The Real Estate Marketplace Glossary: How To Talk The Talk.* (n.d.). ftc.gov. Retrieved January 28, 2024, from https://ftc.gov/ sites/default/files/documents/one-stops/real-estate-compet ion/realestateglossary.pdf

*Studies show better resale value for Energy-Efficient homes.* (n.d.). ENERGY STAR. https://energystar.gov/newhomes/fea tures_benefits/better_resale_value

*House Digest | home improvement, design, DIY, & celebrity interviews.* (n.d.). House Digest. https://housedigest.com/12 7096/how-much-value-smart-devices-add-home/

*Cost vs Value.* (n.d.). Remodeling.net. Retrieved January 28, 2024, from https://www.remodeling.hw.net/cost-vs-value/20 23/